Unsettled...

—Being *in* the World, But Not *of* It—

By,
Margy Hill

Foreward

If there ever was a topic that would exemplify the problems in the 2018 church-world,
1 Peter 2:11-12 would be it! The Lord has called His Church to be set apart from the world but as humans we tend to subtly find our comfort and identity in the world. It's for this reason that the Lord calls us sojourners and pilgrims, and to be at war against the enticements of worldly lusts. In other words, in these last days, He is calling His beloved to be "unsettled" in this life on earth and to be fully satisfied in Him alone.

May the God of all grace strengthen you as learn to be unsettled in this life on earth. May you also find your full worth and identity in Christ for His glory and in His eternal kingdom.

Brad and Diane Lambert
Senior Pastor and Wife
Calvary Chapel Living Hope
Oceanside, California

Study Lessons

How to Study

"Unsettled" is not a study for the faint of heart. It is an opportunity to examine your life in light of the command to be in the world, but not of it.

—Be prepared to be comforted, confronted, and challenged on the journey—

Before you begin each day, it's important to remove all distractions. Set aside enough time to pray, to study the Scriptures, and to respond honestly to the questions. If you commit yourself to the heartwork, you will be forever changed by the time invested.

Each week includes an introductory study focus, with five days of heart work that include a **daily devotion**, and a section to **dig deeper**. Questions are designed to help you understand what Scripture teaches, but also to exhort you to personal examination and application.

For those who are joining others in a small group setting, be sure to allow time to share the study focus, and use the questions to engage in dynamic discussion. Authentic community fosters deep spiritual growth in the lives of every woman involved.

For those who are using this study in the setting of women's Bible Study, there is a wide variety of teaching topics to choose from, many that are not fully addressed in the study. Be creative! Feel free to spread the study out over a longer period of time to focus on key areas, and to give women a platform to share how they are being impacted!

Week 1
Introduction: The Unsettled Life

This world is not my home, I'm just passing through.
My treasures are laid up somewhere beyond the blue.
The angels beckon me from Heaven's open door
And I can't feel at home in this world anymore.

Albert Edward Brumley

Week 1 Introduction: The Unsettled Life

Study Focus

Unsettled…*What kind of response does the word provoke in your mind?*

After ministering on the East Coast for five years, my husband and I returned to Southern California. Our time in Virginia was well spent. God brought many men and women into our lives to disciple, and we deeply loved them. We understood John's pleasure when he wrote:

"I could have no greater joy than to hear that my children are following the truth"

—3 John 1:4

However, the day came when it was clear God was moving us on. It would be difficult to leave behind the relationships and ministry we enjoyed, but we stepped out in faith and obedience to begin a new adventure: *only when we arrived in California, nothing went according to plan*! Everything was in a state of flux: our living situation, our financial situation, our vehicle situation, and our ministry situation. While I desperately searched for *some sort of normal*, it could not be found. After months of trying circumstances, I turned to my husband with tears streaming down and cried:

"I don't know what's wrong – I just feel so unsettled."

Being a loving and compassionate husband, he replied: *"You are supposed to be unsettled."* While I didn't appreciate the lack of sympathy at the time, my husband's words remained in my mind and heart. His gentle rebuke brought a conviction that demanded self-examination. I prayed and turned to the Word of God, ending up in 1st Peter. As I made my way through chapter two, verses eleven and twelve, jumped off the page. I had no idea how powerfully these verses would comfort and challenge me. This study is the result of my discovery. In a nutshell: I needed to be reminded that:

Living the Christian life is living an unsettled life.

We can become so concerned and burdened with what is going on in this life, that we easily forget this world is not our home. There is an incredible tension that must be employed, as we seek to live between two worlds. If we are not careful to search our minds and hearts, we may find ourselves wasting precious moments of our lives, living in futility for this world, instead of fruitfully for the next one.

With that said, I invite you to dig deep into 1st Peter 2:11-12 with me. Be vulnerable and allow the Word of God to change you. I don't know what season of life that you find yourself in as you begin this study, but I guarantee you, God wants to shake up the "settled" places in your life! I am praying for you!

Love from your fellow sojourner,

Margy

Day 1: Defining the Term

Daily Devotion

This world is not our home; but if the truth be told; we can be guilty of living like it is. It's quite easy to grow comfortable and *settle in*. Remarkably, when God brings change into our lives, we resist and fight to protect what we wrongly believe is ours. We quickly forget that Christianity is all about *uncertainty* and *change*. These are features that framed the lives of the great cloud of witnesses who have gone before us. Living *unsettled* is all about embracing the *uncertainty* and *change* that a radical life of faith demands.

If we resist the unsettled life, we will trade a life of impact for a life of mediocrity.

Digging Deeper

1. Look up several definitions and synonyms for the word "unsettled." In what ways do some of these descriptions characterize the Christian life?

   changeable, fickle, fluctuating, uncertain, unpredictable

2. *There is a mind-set in the prosperous West that we deserve a pain-free, trouble-free existence. When life deals us the opposite, we have a right not only to blame somebody or some system and to feel sorry for ourselves, but also to devote most of our time to coping, so that we have no time or energy left over for serving others. This mind-set gives a trajectory to life that is almost universal—namely, away from stress and toward comfort and safety and relief. Then within that very natural trajectory some people begin to think of ministry and find ways of serving God inside the boundaries set by the aims of self-protection. Then churches grow up in this mind-set, and it never occurs to anyone in such a community of believers that choosing discomfort, stress, and danger might be the right thing—even the normal, biblical thing—to do.[i]*

   Living "unsettled" is a *disposition* toward the world that is deeply rooted in biblical truth. However, we must consider if we have adopted the world's mindset. Does the Bible promise believers a life of comfort, safety, and relief? Explain your answer.

   LOL!.... NO!

3. How do you "cope" with the stresses and problems the world is experiencing? Consider your reaction to the news, media and other related sources.

Eating. Numbing w/ TV/shows/movie.

4. How did the apostle Paul describe his life in 2 Corinthians 6:8-10?

"... through honor and dishonor, through slander and praise. We are treated as impostors, and yet they are true; as unknown, and yet well known; as dying, and behold, we live; as punished, and yet not killed; as sorrowful, yet always rejoicing; as poor, yet making many rich; as having nothing, yet possessing everything."

5. Be honest. Based on your introduction to the unsettled life, which life have you embraced more—the settled or unsettled life? Why?

but also forced to

Settled, because that is what I have been desiring; striving for: a steady salary, good benefits, independent, savings, travel, leisure, mild materialism, clinging! searching for spiritual family. All of which aren't necessarily bad things and also been great because my personal circumstances forced me to grow up and be my own adult! parent to self / reach out to spiritual family. However, on the topic of "change", God stripped me of everything above for a reason. To teach me to even then, that all isn't forever! Something I should live for, only Him. Here in the relational desert of San Diego. .... and also being released unexpectedly from the job I moved out here for.

10

Day 2: Restless Pilgrim

Daily Devotion

If we were to assign our own title to the Book of First Peter, "Restless Pilgrim" would be a good choice. Peter is the author. He identifies believers as sojourners and pilgrims (1 Peter 2:11-12) and is concerned about their conduct during the time of their stay here on earth (1 Peter 1:17). Here and throughout Scripture, we recognize a common theme:

> ***Christians are temporary visitors who are awaiting their return to their true homeland: heaven.***

Peter is writing to Jewish and Gentile Christians who were scattered throughout Asia Minor. Many scholars believe the book was written just prior to the persecutions of Nero, which began in A.D. 64. However, persecutions had already begun in some parts of the Roman Empire, and in Rome in particular.

If "Babylon" is used symbolically for the Roman capital (1 Peter 5:13), it is likely 1st Peter was probably written in A.D. 63-64. It is important to understand the environment Christians were living in. Their "unsettled" circumstances would make it difficult to obey Peter's challenge to live godly lives in the midst of ongoing pagan hostility. Instead of mourning their losses, Peter's encouragement is to focus on, and rejoice in, the glory to come.

Digging Deeper

1. Take some time to enjoy and read the Book of 1 Peter. According to verses 1:1, 1:17, and 2:11 how does Peter describe the believer's identity?

2. What kind of lifestyle does Peter call believers to live in 1 Peter 1:14-16?

3. Eight verses in this book refer to the topic of suffering. Write a paragraph on suffering based on your understanding of these verses (1:11, 2:19, 3:13, 3:18, 4:12, 4:13, 5:1, 5:9).

4. There are two key verses in the book of 1st Peter that will serve as our foundation, guide map, and instructions for our journey together. Read and write out 1 Peter 2:11-12.

5. Describe what you think it means to be a "restless pilgrim."

Day 3: Blind Spots

Daily Devotion

The term "blind spot" is not unfamiliar. It's an area in our life that needs attention, but we can't see it. Although the term cannot be found in the Bible, the principle is taught in Psalm 19:12-13:

> "Who can understand his errors? Cleanse me from secret faults. Keep back Your servant also from presumptuous sins; let them not have dominion over me. Then I shall be blameless, and I shall be innocent of great transgression."

Is it possible the greatest blind spot today in American Christianity is the pursuit of comfort? Do we ever take inventory or examine our lives to see if we have become too "settled" in the world? Has comfort become such a near and dear friend, that we don't recognize it can also be our worst enemy? Let's take an honest evaluation of where we are currently at in our walks with Christ, in order to pray and allow this study to have its full work in our lives.

Digging Deeper

1. Look up the word "cynical" in a dictionary and record a few definitions and synonyms. In short, you might say being cynical is always expecting the worst: *in circumstances and in people*. You may be surprised that becoming a cynical Christian begins with familiarity. The word "familiar" means "well known" or "close association." It is also defined as "in close friendship" or "intimate". The word "familiar" and "comfortable" are actually synonyms of one another. Unfortunately, the believer's familiarity with the world can breed contempt for the world. Instead of seeing the world's need for Christ, cynical Christians become critics of the world who play a consistent drumbeat of condemnation.

   Read and write out John 3:17. Why did Jesus come to the world?

2. Instead of being players on Christ's team to save the world, cynical Christians have become referees on the field, calling attention to every penalty. Do you find yourself grumbling and criticizing the unbelieving world, more than praying and sharing with the unbelieving world? Why or why not?

3. Pride, judgmentalism, a critical spirit, and whining and complaining, are just a few of the blind spots that can be overlooked in the Christian life. God has called us to love the world. That is why we are here. Life is not about us— consider Jonah. His response to the salvation of the Ninevites is less than celebratory. How did he react according to Jonah 4:1-3?

4. Blind spots occur when we fail to daily subject ourselves to the Word of God. What do we learn about the importance of the Word of God and its application to our lives in James 1:21-27?

5. We have a front row seat to the sin of the world—Lot did too. He chose to live with his family in the gates of Sodom. 2 Peter 4:7 records he was "oppressed by the filthy conduct of the wicked," but to our knowledge it appears his life was just that—*oppressed*. How should the believer in Christ view the unbelieving world? Use Scripture to support your answer.

Day 4: The Lord is My Portion

Daily Devotion

Imagine a life of faith! Because we are not settlers in this land, and because we know our great and awesome God, we can journey through life embracing the unknown. Living an unsettled life is uncomfortable. An unsettled life requires that we surrender our plans for God's plans. An unsettled life requires our humility, trusting that God's way is better than our own. Yes, the unsettled life is filled with uncertainty, but it delivers a life of impact. It brings with it a deep and meaningful joy that comes from knowing and believing in the faithfulness of God. He is our portion!

Digging Deeper

1. Take a moment to consider the "unsettled" life. How do you think it might impact these key areas in your daily walk?

    - Temptation and Sanctification

    - Responding to Persecution

    - Perseverance in Suffering

    - Witnessing to the World

2. Read Psalm 73. Asaph sees injustice all around him. He remembers that he is only a pilgrim on earth. He has an inheritance—a portion—that is greater than any wealth the wicked possess. His portion is God Himself. What does it mean to you to have God as your portion?

3. Read Lamentations 3:21-24. Why is this reminder so vital on the journey?

4. As we dig deeper into the "unsettled" life, it is a good time to evaluate where you might be misplacing your hope. Hope deferred makes the heart sick (Proverbs 13:12). Where have you been most disappointed in this life? What have you hoped in to overcome?

5. So the choice is yours—settled or unsettled? Which will you choose and why?

Day 5: Living Unsettled

1. Which of the four days this week challenged you the most?

2. Write a paragraph summarizing what you have learned about the unsettled life.

3. What key verse will you seek to memorize and hide in your heart?

4. Moving forward, how will you apply what you have learned?

5. Take some time to consider your answers and compose a prayer that reflects what God's Word has spoken to you.

Week 2
Beloved
1 Peter 2:11

So nigh, so very nigh to God,
I cannot nearer be;
For in the person of His Son
I am as near as He.

So dear, so very dear to God,
More dear I cannot be;
The love wherewith He loves the Son,
Such is His love to me.

A Mind at Perfect Peace with God
Horatius Bonar 1847

Week 2: Beloved

Beloved —1 Peter 2:11

Study Focus

At the heart of the "unsettled" life, lies the precious truth that we are God's *beloved*. Peter uses this word to ensure his readers of his love for them, but beyond the apostle's love, the term would call to mind the truth of God's love. The exhortation to live the Christian life is based on love. It is difficult to fathom that God loves us with the same infinite love he has for his Son.

If we are to thrive in the challenges a life of faith brings, we must be certain that the One who is sovereign over all deeply loves us.

The word *beloved* is an adjective that means "greatly loved or dear to the heart". When used as a noun, it refers to a person who is "dearly loved", "esteemed", "favorite", or "worthy of love". The word *beloved* speaks of the one who is being loved, never of the one doing the loving. The One doing the loving is the God of the universe who has chosen to love you. You and I may never fully comprehend the love of God, but we can be encouraged that we have been called *beloved* and our response is merely to ***be loved***.

Consider all the comforts of life that you now enjoy: a roof over your head, a car to drive, a job that provides, a church where you belong, and close relationships with family and friends. If you trust that you are God's beloved, you need not fear losing anything or anyone in this life, because nothing can separate you from the love of God. His perfect love casts out all fear. You are now and will always be His beloved.

Peter is about to issue a serious challenge to those he is writing to. Believers in Asia Minor were suffering from escalating persecution. The purpose of Peter's letter is to instruct them regarding how to live victoriously in the midst of ongoing hostility. He is going to command these Christians who are living under great duress, to live a godly life, and evangelize the lost. It would not be easy to obey. Without the knowledge of God's great love, fear would continually be an obstacle to living as God has commanded.

If we are confident in the love of our Heavenly Father, we can live boldly for His purposes, trusting Him in every facet of our lives. Although, He calls us to be "unsettled" in this life, we remain "settled" in the knowledge of His love.

Day 1: The Father's Love

Daily Devotion

How deep the Father's love for us

How vast beyond all measure

That He should give His only Son

To make a wretch His treasure

How great the pain of searing loss

The Father turns His face away

As wounds which mar the Chosen One

Bring many sons to glory

Behold the man upon a cross

My sin upon His shoulders

Ashamed, I hear my mocking voice

Call out among the scoffers

It was my sin that held Him there

Until it was accomplished

His dying breath has brought me life

I know that it is finished

I will not boast in anything

No gifts, no power, no wisdom

But I will boast in Jesus Christ

His death…

Stuart Townend

Digging Deeper

1. Read and write out 1 John 3:1. How do the words of this famous hymn reveal the depth of the Father?

2. John tells us to "behold" the manner of love that God bestows upon His children. In the Greek, this word means to pay attention or observe! Using Psalm 103:1-10 to inspire you, describe the love God lavishes upon believers.

3. God calls Himself "Father" because the word characterizes His relationship with us better than any other word. How would you describe God as your Father?

4. Is it difficult for you to receive the Father's love? Why or why not?

5. It is not uncommon to personally fail to grasp God's love or doubt it. What are some of the thoughts below that have caused you difficulty. Take some time to comment.

    *   Insisting you must be worthy of God's love.

    *   Doubting God's love due to your pain and suffering or the pain and suffering of others?

    *   Living with a superficial understanding of the greatness of God's love.

    *   Your Own Response:

    Describe some ways you can get to better know your Father's love.

Day 2: Perfect Love

Daily Devotion

Read John 4:7-21.

Sadly, there are many professed Christians who fear death above all things. Yet John is preaching that "perfect love casts out fear." Those who cling to life and beg for their lives in life-threatening situations ought to ask themselves why. Are they fearful of God's judgment? Do they love this world so much that they do not wish to leave? Do they fear that leaving loved ones behind is too much for God to handle? It is inborn to fear natural disasters, diseases, germs, and suffering, but isn't God sovereign over all of these? Of course! Therefore, if perfect love casts out fear, let us as God's people make certain that we fear nothing this world can throw at us. If our time on earth is known to God—from the day of our birth to the day of our death—what is there to fear for those who love God? Nothing! In fact, every single day is worth rejoicing in, for the love of God is being perfected in us, making us more and more holy. As we watch God work in our lives, let us therefore rejoice in what He is doing, even when it's painful. Let us be diligent to love our brothers in Christ with the love of Christ, forgiving those who have offended us, letting go of bitterness towards those who have hurt us, and making amends by repenting of our shortcomings and sins. It is not only to the glory of God that we do so, it is for our sanctification and perfection, and also for our own joy.[ii]

Digging Deeper

1. Why is God's love "perfect" as compared to "imperfect"?

2. According to 1 John 4:9-10, and Romans 5:6-8, how does God demonstrate His love for you?

3. Focus on 1 John 4:12-16. If you are unable to see God, what is the evidence of His love in you?

4. Why is God's perfect love able to cast out fear 1 John 4:18?

5. What do you fear the most?

Day 3: Trust In God Only

Daily Devotion

God does not willingly bring affliction or grief to us. He does not delight in causing us to experience pain or heartache. He always has a purpose for the grief He brings or allows to come into our lives. Most often we do not know what that purpose is, but it is enough to know that His infinite wisdom and perfect love have determined that the particular sorrow is best for us. God never wastes pain. He always uses it to accomplish His purpose. And His purpose is for His glory and our good. Therefore, we can trust Him when our hearts are aching or our bodies are racked with pain.[iii]

Digging Deeper

1. Do you find it difficult to trust God in times of pain and sorrow? Why or why not?

2. Read Psalm 62. The psalmist says that his soul finds rest in God alone, and that God alone is his rock, his salvation and his fortress. What does this tell you about the faith of the psalmist?

3. What kind of things do you tend to look for peace in, or trust as your security and your firm foundation?

4. What does it mean to trust God as your rock, your refuge, your fortress?

5. In what area of your life do you find it difficult to trust God? What would be different if you decided to turn this area of your life over to God?

Day 4: Living in the Tension

Daily Devotion

The tension of living between two worlds is real. These are good and necessary tensions; and they shouldn't lead to discouragement, despair, hopelessness, or depression. If you are experiencing these tensions of the Christian life, there is a reason: you are a pilgrim on the way. In fact, you are only a sojourner in this land with eyes that have been set upon the "celestial city." As Christians, we are caught in the in-between. As has become a common refrain (and Jesus alludes to in His high priestly prayer), "We are in this world, but not of this world." We have one foot on earth and one firmly anchored in heaven. When we begin to fully understand that we are but pilgrims in this world, these tensions become avenues of sweetness rather than despair. Ultimately, they point us to what we shall be some day.[iv]

- We are set free from sin yet continue to yield to it (Rom. 6:2; Rom. 7:19)
- We are saints yet sinners (1 Cor. 1:2; 1 John 1:8)
- We have peace yet are to strive for peace (Eph. 2:14; Col. 3:15)
- We have been saved yet are to work out our salvation with fear and trembling (Eph. 2:8; Phil. 2:12)
- We are beautiful yet wretched (Song of Sol. 4:1; Rom. 7:24)
- We have been given rest yet are to labor to enter that rest (Matt. 11:28; Heb. 4:11)
- We are forgiven yet continue to need to confess sin (Col. 3:13; 1 John 1:9)
- We know the love of Christ yet this love surpasses our knowledge (Ps. 89:1; Eph. 3:19)
- We have died to sin yet must continue to flee from it (Rom. 6:2; 1 Cor. 6:18)
- We are new yet we are not what we shall be (John 3:3; 1 John 3:2)
- We have seen Him yet have not seen Him (Eph. 1:18; 1 Pet. 1:8)
- We have all knowledge yet are to increase in knowing Him (1 John 2:20; 2 Pet. 3:18)
- We are a new creation yet battle the old self (2 Cor. 5:17; Rom. 6:6)
- We have joy yet we are commanded to rejoice (Gal. 5:22; Phil. 4:4)
- We have been set free yet are slaves (Rom. 6:18; Rom. 6:22)
- We are fallen creatures and yet sons of God (Rom. 3:12; Gal. 4:6)

Digging Deeper

1. As you consider the above tensions in the Christian life, add a few of your own.

2. Which of the above tensions or one that you added, do you most struggle with?

3. We love to rely on the promises of God, yet we conveniently overlook the difficulty that is promised in the Christian life. Look up the following verses and fill in the blanks.

- In the world you will have _____ but be of good cheer, I have overcome the world (John 16:33).

- For to you it has been granted on behalf of Christ, not only to believe in Him, but also to _____ for His sake (Philippians 1:29).

- Yes, and all who desire to live godly in Christ Jesus will _____ _____ (2 Timothy 3:12).

- Beloved, do not think it _____ concerning the fiery trial which is to try you, as though some _____ thing happened to you (1 Peter 4:12).

4. How does the promise of 1 Peter 5:10 encourage you?

5. While we live "unsettled" lives, we remain "settled" in God's love. This is the secret to living in the tension. Share an "unsettled" moment in your life where you remained "settled" in His love.

Day 5: Living Unsettled

1. Which of the four days this week challenged you the most?

2. Write a paragraph summarizing what you have learned about the unsettled life.

3. What key verse will you seek to memorize and hide in your heart?

4. Moving forward, how will you apply what you have learned?

5. Take some time to consider your answers and compose a prayer that reflects what God's Word has spoken to you.

Week 3
Sojourners and Pilgrims
1 Peter 2:11

A pilgrim and a stranger,
I journey here below;
Far distant is my country,
The home to which I go.
Here I must toil and travail,
Oft weary and opprest,
But there my God shall lead me
To everlasting rest.

Paul Gerhardt 1666
A Pilgrim and a Stranger

Week 3: Sojourners and Pilgrims

Beloved, I beg you as sojourners and pilgrims—1 Peter 2:11

Study Focus

In order to live unsettled lives, it is imperative that we think of ourselves in light of our true identity: *sojourners and pilgrims*. It is on the basis of this reality, that Peter makes his appeal. The word "sojourner" (*paroikos)*, and the word "pilgrim" (*parepidemos*) are adjectives which describe, "A person who for a period of time lives in a place which is not his normal residence—'alien, stranger, temporary resident.'" [v]

While the person lives among the citizens of a land, he is not a citizen himself. Even though he may have received the legal status to live in the land, he doesn't have the same right to participate in society as does a legal citizen. By using these words, Peter reminds his readers (and us) that they are no longer citizens of the world. Even though they live in the midst of the world, they are now heavenly citizens, and therefore cannot participate in the activities of a lost world as they once did. *They must learn to live among those in the world without being like them.*

In other words, believers must embrace the mindset of sojourners and pilgrims. They are to adopt an attitude of a temporary traveler who is merely passing through a certain territory on the way to his final destination. Thomas Constable wrote: "Christians if they rightly consider their calling, must never settle themselves here, but feel themselves travelers."

While sermons on pilgrimage are not popular today, the topic was widely preached by saints of old. In September of 1733, Jonathan Edwards (1703-1758) preached a sermon called "The Christian Pilgrim" or "The True Christian's Life a Journey toward Heaven" based on the truths found in Hebrews 11:13:

> *These all died in faith, not having received the promises, but having seen them afar off were assured of them, embraced them and confessed that they were strangers and pilgrims on the earth.*

The Old Testament saints confessed and declared their alien status. They understood they were just passing through this world on their way to their true country and homeland. This week we will embrace the pilgrim mindset by studying the seven principles Jonathan Edwards shared in his 1733 sermon.

Day 1: Pilgrim Principle #1: Don't get comfortable.

Daily Devotion

A traveler is not enticed by fine appearances to put off the thought of proceeding. No, but his journey's end is in his mind. If he meets with comfortable accommodations at an inn, he entertains no thoughts of settling there. He considers that these things are not his own, that he is but a stranger, and when he has refreshed himself, or tarried for a night, he is for going forward – Jonathan Edwards

Living radically for Christ is never going to be comfortable. The truth of the matter is it's not supposed to be. Being uncomfortable and suffering for Christ is the cost of following Him. Stepping out of our comfort zones and into His will for our lives is what He desires. Consider the lives of the Old Testament saints.

- *Praying in public took Daniel from the comfort of his home to a den full of hungry lions.*
- *Worshiping only God took Shadrach, Meshach, and Abednego from the comforts of security, to the burning fiery furnace and anger of a king.*
- *Faithfulness to God took Mary from the comfort of an ideal life to being a pregnant un-wed girl delivering God's own Son in a barn.*
- *Following God took Moses from the comfort of shepherding a few sheep to leading the Israelites in a desert to the Promised Land for forty years.*
- *Obedience to God took Abraham from the comfort of his hometown to an unknown land.*
- *Faith took Esther from the comfort of her castle to the scepter and possible rejection of her king.*
- *Trusting God took David from the comfort of shepherding sheep in the fields to the battlefield and then to the throne of a king.*
- *Love took Jesus from the comforts of heaven to the pain of the cross.[vi]*

Digging Deeper

1. God has blessed His people with many things to enjoy on the journey. What are some of the everyday comforts you enjoy?

2. What are some of the dangers of becoming too comfortable?

3. Why do you think some Christians today believe they are entitled to live comfortable lives?

4. Where are you most comfortable in your life? Do you see your desire for comfort as a danger to your life of faith? Why or why not?

5. Explain how a resistance to change can be a resistance to spiritual growth.

Day 2: Pilgrim Principle #2: Loosen your grip.

Daily Devotion

So should we desire heaven more than the comforts and enjoyments of this life? Our hearts ought to be loose to these things, as that of a man on a journey, that we may as cheerfully part with them whenever God calls – Jonathan Edwards

Relevant Magazine published an article in May of 2015 called *The Art of Holding Loosely*. The author identified the real problem as it relates to our mindset towards worldly things:

Somewhere around the age of two or three, kids learn a word that often becomes one of their favorites. It's a word that defines people and things and places and life—and later, it can delineate or destroy a person's life: "Mine." Mine seems simple, but it really isn't. There is an "I'm-in-control" attitude that comes along with that word. We live in a "me-saturated" culture. The problem with this is that, not only is it self-centered and self-focused, in reality, this *mine* business is a false construct. It gives us a fake sense of security that leads to a white-knuckled grip on the steering wheel of life. We hold tight to what we deem is ours. Of course, we know in theory that everything belongs to God, but we still cling tightly to the idea that we can be in control of our own lives. But in actuality, we can't control our lives. [vii]

Digging Deeper

1. Learning to hold loosely to the things of this world is key to the pilgrim life. Read Mark 4:13-19. Write out Mark 4:19.

2. What does Mark mean when he refers to the *cares of this world*, the *deceitfulness of riches*, and the *desires for other things*?

   - Cares of this world

   - Deceitfulness of riches

   - Desires for other things

33

3. In what ways does the world continually appeal to our desires for more?

4. We seldom recognize if we are on holding on to tightly to something, until we are threatened with it being taken away. Is there anything in your life that you fear losing? Explain your answer.

5. Read Matthew 6:19-21. Where is your treasure? Where is your heart?

Day 3: Pilgrim Principle #3: Pilgrims aim at Christlikeness.

Daily Devotion

We should be endeavoring to come nearer to heaven, in being more heavenly, becoming more and more like the inhabitants of heaven in respect of holiness and conformity to God, the knowledge of God and Christ, in clear views of the glory of God, the beauty of Christ, and the excellency of divine things, as we come nearer to the beatific vision. We should labor to be continually growing in divine love. That this may be an increasing flame in our hearts, till they ascend wholly in this flame – Jonathan Edwards

Does heaven have a hold on you? C.S. Lewis was correct when he said "Aim at heaven and you will get earth thrown in. Aim at earth and you get neither." Aiming at heaven also involves keeping Jesus in our sights. Looking forward to the day when "we shall see Him as He is" fills us with hope—not a worldly, wish-list kind of hope, but a hope that reflects the certainty of what is to come. It's the kind of hope that keeps us from distractions and rivets our attention on what really matters in the long run; the kind of hope that purifies us.

Digging Deeper

1. Read John 3:1-3. Write out John 3:3

2. In what ways should a heavenly focus stir your heart to purity? Use Scripture to support your answer.

Pilgrim Principle #4: Pilgrims find their satisfaction in God.

God is the highest good of the reasonable creature, and the enjoyment of Him is the only happiness with which our souls can be satisfied. To go to heaven fully to enjoy God, is infinitely better than the most pleasant accommodations here. Fathers and mothers, husbands, wives, children, or the company of earthly friends, are but shadows. But the enjoyment of God is the substance. These are but scattered beams, but God is the sun. These are but streams, but God is the fountain. These are but drops, but God is the ocean. . . . Why should we labor for, or set our hearts on anything else, but that which is our proper end, and true happiness? – Jonathan Edwards

Are you envious of the lives your friends are living as you scroll through Facebook? Maybe it's a new car they purchased, or a glamourous vacation spot they chose to visit, or maybe the perfect family photos they continue to post. You assume all is well in their life, but what about yours? You find yourself completely dissatisfied with your life. True satisfaction cannot be found in the temporary things of the world. Outside of Christ, satisfaction cannot be found, only continually sought after. God is the only One who can satisfy.

3. Read Psalm 42. How does your life resonate with that of the psalmist?

4. What did Jesus say to the woman at the well in John 4:13-14?

5. In what people or things have you tried to find satisfaction?

Day 4: Pilgrim Principle #5: No Fear

Daily Devotion

To spend our lives so as to be only a journeying towards heaven, is the way to be free from bondage and to have the prospect and forethought of death comfortable. Does the traveler think of his journey's end with fear and terror? Is it terrible to him to think that he has almost got to his journey's end? Were the children of Israel sorry after forty years' travel in the wilderness, when they had almost got to Canaan? – Jonathan Edwards

Digging Deeper

1. Read Philippians 1:21. Why could Paul say to "die is gain."

2. Do you have any fear of death? Why or why not?

Pilgrim Principle #6: Pilgrims ponder what they pursue.

Labor to be much acquainted with heaven. - If you are not acquainted with it, you will not be likely to spend your life as a journey thither. You will not be sensible of its worth, nor will you long for it. Unless you are much conversant in your mind with a better good, it will be exceeding difficult to you to have your hearts loose from these things, to use them only in subordination to something else, and be ready to part with them for the sake of that better good. - Labor therefore to obtain a realizing sense of a heavenly world, to get a firm belief of its reality, and to be very much conversant with it in your thoughts —Jonathan Edwards

3. What does Philippians 3:17-21 teach concerning the believer's citizenship?

4. Do you tend to view heavenly citizenship as a future promise rather than a present reality? Why or why not?

Pilgrim Principle #7 Pilgrims travel together.

Let Christians help one another in going this journey. . . . Company is very desirable in a journey, but in none so much as this. - Let them go united and not fall out by the way, which would be to hinder one another, but use all means they can to help each other up the hill. - This would ensure a more successful traveling and a more joyful meeting at their Father's house in glory—Jonathan Edwards

5. Read Hebrews 10:23-25. Who are your fellow companions on your journey? Are you surrounding yourself with those who are running their race to win? Why or why not?

Day 5: Living Unsettled

1. Which of the four days this week challenged you the most?

2. Write a paragraph summarizing what you have learned about the unsettled life.

3. What key verse will you seek to memorize and hide in your heart?

4. Moving forward, how will you apply what you have learned?

5. Take some time to consider your answers and compose a prayer that reflects what God's Word has spoken to you.

Week 4
Separation Not Isolation

Set apart for our God above
Set apart for the One we love
Set apart for Your glory

Set Apart
Tim Hughes

Week 4: Separation Not Isolation

Study Focus

The Bible refers to believers as "peculiar" people. As we have learned, we are not citizens of this world, and our purpose for being here is to make Christ known. Our life is to look very different from the life of the unbeliever, and we are to live different lives to make a difference in the world. The "set apart" life requires a strong, biblical worldview. A worldview simply defined is: The overall perspective through which one sees and interprets the world. It is a collection of beliefs about life, culture, and the universe held by an individual or a group. A *biblical* worldview is:

> *Seeing and interpreting the world according to the Word of God, allowing it to have full authority in our lives — which means believing it is entirely true, and allowing it to serve as the foundation of everything we say and do.*

With this foundation in place, it is easy for the believer in Christ to live in the world, yet understand their separation from it. They approach life knowing: "Christianity is not merely religious truth, it is total truth—truth about the whole of reality (Francis Schaefer)." However, without this foundation, a believer may fear living in the world and actually isolate from it, in order to avoid any type of interaction with those who do not believe.

In addition, there is the case of the believer who is more informed by the world, than the Word of God. Research suggests that American Christianity struggles in its attempt to live out a biblical worldview. George Barna summarizes: "*Most Americans have little idea how to integrate core biblical principles to form a unified and meaningful response to the challenges and opportunities of life. Most people don't consider their worldview to be a central element of their life, although it is.*

If believers do not adopt a biblical orientation, they will end up orientating their lives according to the world. Orientation orders the thoughts, informs the thinking and conforms practices to a common standard. If the Word of God is not providing the orientation, believers who are meant to stand out in the culture, will end up merely blending in.

So where do you find yourself today? Are you hiding and isolating from the world? Are you blending in? Or are you standing out— do people notice there is something different about you? Sojourners and pilgrims have a purpose for their time here on earth. They are called to be ambassadors of Christ.

Do you have a biblical worldview? Do you agree with God about everything? Do you believe in traditional marriage being one man and one woman? Do you agree with God in His pro-life position? Do you believe in biblical womanhood and the roles God has blessed women with? How you answer these questions will directly impact your influence in the world – whether you *hide away, blend in, or stand out.*

This week we will study what we are to be doing on our journey. If we forget the reason we are here, we will find ourselves "settled" for this life.

Day 1: Bubble Wrapped

Daily Devotion

Christians are not to live in a bubble.

"By "Christian bubble" I mean the subculture Christians create that allows us to conduct our entire life having minimal contact with anything "secular." Bubble residents choose their activities based on where they can be with other Christians—from small groups, to play dates, to basketball leagues. The "world" is viewed as something to be avoided. The Christian bubble can quickly envelop almost every aspect of life…The Christian bubble can destroy our passion to a part of Christ's mission."[viii]

It's time to pop the bubble. More than ever before, the world needs to see authentic Christianity lived out. To live biblically, doesn't mean we beat people over the head with our Bible. The call is to make Christ known in the world, find ways to building bridges in understanding the culture, and share the good news of the gospel of Jesus Christ. This idea leaves many of us "unsettled" but it presents an opportunity to trust God as we radically live out our faith.

Digging Deeper

1. Read Matthew 5:13-16 and using your own words, summarize with a paragraph.

2. What two concerns does Jesus address in these verses?

3. Identify your biggest fear in sharing your faith with the unbelieving world. What are some ways you might seek to overcome it?

4. How are you encouraged by the following verses to witness to the world about Christ?

- Matthew 5:11-12

- Luke 12:11-12

- Romans 1:16

- 1 Corinthians 3:5-8

5. What does Jesus mean by saltiness? How does a Christian lose their "flavor"?

Day 2: A lot like Lot

Daily Devotion
Study Genesis 19 and 2 Peter 2:4-10.

It is hard to reconcile Lot's life. Peter is clear to tell us that Lot is saved (2 Peter 2:7), but we wonder why he spent his life in Sodom.

Righteous Lot loved Sodom. While scandalized by it, he hung on to it for dear life. And he and his family paid dearly. So listen carefully. Setting ourselves apart from the world so that we might reach the world is not so much a series of no's as much as it is an immense yes to Christ and all that He gives. Ironically, though Lot was revolted by Sodom, Sodom was in his soul. It is possible, then, for a believer to be oppressed by the world while willfully clinging to the world. There is every evidence that righteous Lot was of no benefit whatsoever to the inhabitants of Sodom. Though he lived in Sodom for years and was prominent in its gates, and therefore would have had many opportunities to influence his friends, Lot utterly disappointed.

In 2 Peter 2:4-10, Peter is not pointing to Lot as an example of separated living, but rather as a stunning example of God's grace. Even though Lot was saved and deemed righteous, his life on earth was of no consequence. He lived in the world and became a part of it.

Sodom influenced Lot more than Lot influenced Sodom.

Digging Deeper

1. Read 1 Corinthians 3:10-15. Do you think verse 15 applies to Lot? Why or why not?

2. Read Luke 17:28-33. What did Jesus say about Lot's wife?

3. Lot's lifestyle and his choice to live in Sodom put his family at risk. What choice did Lot's wife make that determined her fate?

4. We do not know why Lot persisted in living in Sodom, when its wickedness so distressed him. But he allowed that distress to have the final say. While believers should be saddened by the sin they see in the world, what should be their response be to it?

5. Read Ephesians 5:8-16. How should believers live in light of the sin in the world?

Day 3: A Standout

Daily Devotion

Does the news make you angry? Do you believe that evil is triumphing over good? Do you find it difficult to maintain a heart of love toward the unbelieving world? If you answered with a "yes" to any of those questions, you recognize the challenge of living as a *standout* in the world. You have been called to walk a fine line. Because this world is not your home, you find yourself unsettled and disturbed in this world, and rightly so. But because God has asked you to be in the world, you must choose to be a standout for Him. He does not want you to *hide away* in the bubble, He does not want you to *blend in* the world like Lot. He wants you to *stand out* in the world representing Christ and serving as a minister of reconciliation to the lost and the hurting. If we want to *stand out* we need to be sure of who we are, why we are here and where our help comes from.

Digging Deeper

1. Share some of what you see going on in the world that causes you to lose hope.

2. Why is it important that we keep in mind the truth of 2 Corinthians 4:18 and Hebrews 11:1 in mind?

3. How did Daniel know when to take a bold stand and when to be more diplomatic and polite? Use Scripture to support your answer.

4. What is the believer's responsibility in conducting themselves as a witness to the world according to Colossians 4:5-6?

5. Describe a recent challenge you encountered in sharing your faith.

Day 4: Semper Gumby

Daily Devotion

Always flexible. "Semper Gumby" is the unofficial motto for the U.S. Military Services and it certainly applies to sojourners and pilgrims. God has called us to represent Him in the world and is continually desiring to *stretch* us in our faith. His leading will often be inconvenient and interrupt our plans. Often we can resist the prompting of the Holy Spirit, being unwilling to *bend* to His will. Learning to be flexible in our everyday lives can bring spontaneity and excitement as we become intentional in welcoming unexpected opportunities that pop up in our day.

Philip would definitely win the "Semper Gumby" award. While he is not an apostle, New Testament author, or leader in the church, he is known for his obedience to share Christ wherever God sent Him.

Digging Deeper

1. Read Acts 8:4-8. Describe Philip's ministry in Samaria.

2. "And there was great joy in that city (Acts 8:8)." Share the last time you experienced great joy when God used you to share your faith.

3. What do you notice about Philip in Acts 8:26-40? In what ways are you impacted by his example?

4. Philip was prepared to answer the Eunuch's question. Are you prepared to answer questions regarding what you believe? Why or why not?

5. What are some steps you can take to better equipped to evangelize and disciple others?

Day 5: Living Unsettled

1. Which of the four days this week challenged you the most?

2. Write a paragraph summarizing what you have learned about the unsettled life.

3. What key verse will you seek to memorize and hide in your heart?

4. Moving forward, how will you apply what you have learned?

5. Take some time to consider your answers and compose a prayer that reflects what God's Word has spoken to you.

Week 5
Waging War
1 Peter 2:12

Guide me, O Thou great Jehovah,
Pilgrim through this barren land;
I am weak, but Thou art mighty,
Hold me with Thy powerful hand.

Guide Me, O Thou Great Jehovah
William Williams 1745

Week 5: Waging War

Abstain from fleshly lusts which war against the soul—1 Peter 2:11

Study Focus

Because believers are merely passing through this world, they cannot afford to become entrenched in the world. They must wage war by abstaining from fleshly lusts which surround them on all sides. The word "abstain" is the Greek word *apechomai*, which means to:

- *Deliberately withdraw from*
- *To stay away from*
- *To put distance between oneself and something else*
- *To intentionally abstain.*

When Peter speaks of "fleshly lusts," he uses the word *sarkikos* for "fleshly." This word describes the impulses, cravings, and desires of the carnal flesh — those things that appeal to our baser instincts. The word "lusts" is the word *epithumia*, a compound of the words *epi* and *thumos*. The word *epi* means "over," and the word *thumos* depicts "passion". When compounded into the word *epithumia*: *It pictures a person so overcome by some passionate desire that he completely gives himself over to it.*

Your flesh is never satisfied until it completely takes over and consumes you. The war is a fierce one. The flesh seeks to dominate and control your entire life. Sin may be pleasurable for a season, but we are foolish to think we can dabble in it, and not be conquered by it.

This is why Peter pleads with us, based on our identity as sojourners and pilgrims, to "abstain from fleshly lusts, which war against the soul." The word "war" is the Greek word *strateuomai*. This word is derived from the word *stratos*, from which we get the word *strategy*. But when it becomes the word *strateuomai* as used in this context, it describes the flesh as *a fiercely committed soldier who possesses a warring mentality.* Because the flesh is so committed to waging war and destroying his resistance, he fights tactically, strategically, and aggressively. Furthermore, the Greek tense accentuates the fact that once the flesh has been allowed to express itself, it will wage *continual warfare* and its assault will be *unending*.

Peter's chief concern is that the flesh will wage continual warfare against the "soul." The word "soul" is the Greek word *psyche*, which describes *a person's mind, will, and emotions.* The New Testament writers clearly understood that the mind, will, and emotions are where Satan wages his greatest warfare against the saints. Therefore, Peter urges his readers not to open the door and invite this warfare to begin by deliberately participating in sinful activities. Instead, he tells them to abstain from fleshly lusts, thus keeping their mind, will, and emotions free of unnecessary battles.

Peter's words in First Peter 2:11 could be interpreted to mean: *"Dearly beloved, I sincerely beg and warn you to live as if you are travelers here in this world. Never forget that this is not your real residence and that you must not become too attached to the environment around you. I urge you to refrain from any carnal, low-level desires that try to engulf you and thus drag you into a very long, protracted, strategic, and aggressive war in your mind, will, and emotions."*[ix]

Day 1: It's Tempting!

Daily Devotion

You may reminder the clever dare included in the Lay's Potato Chip advertising campaign: "Bet you can't eat just one!" The slogan resonated with thousands of viewers, because it was true. It's a real struggle to eat just one chip. You open the bag and before you know it, you've eaten the whole bag. The world we live in offers us a taste of every variety of sinful activity, and the enemy is hoping we will not only sample it once, but over and over again. What may appear at first to be a harmless choice, can actually lead to destruction.

Digging Deeper

1. What do you learn about sin in James 1:12-15?

2. When believers are tempted; they are drawn away by their own desires. What are some desires that may not necessarily be bad in and of themselves, but can cause the believer to adopt them as an idol, or even worse, become addicted?

3. Share a time in your past when you allowed yourself to dabble in a little sin? How did that one decision lead to a pattern of sin?

4. If you were counseling a woman who was being tempted to engage in some type of sin, what helpful advice would you give her to help her abstain? Use Scripture to support your answer.

5. Is there one particular sin you are struggling with right now? Are there places or people you need to avoid in order to stay free? Explain your answer.

Day 2: Culture and the Christian

Daily Devotion

Today, it is not unusual to meet people who claim to be Christians, but in all reality are more defined by the culture, then they are by Christ. Many pay lip service to the existence of God, but they don't live as if He exists. Their beliefs include syncretistic ideologies that are a mixture of some of what the Bible teaches, and those beliefs commonly held by the culture. In other words, *it's cool to be a Christian when it works for personal benefit*. It might be said that they are quite at home in this world, and love what it has to offer. This begs the question, is it possible to love the world and love Christ?

Digging Deeper

1. Read 1 John 4:15-17. Is it possible to love the world and Christ? Why or why not?

2. What are some of the dangers of loving the world?

3. Give some practical examples of what John is writing about:

   - The lust of the flesh

   - The lust of the eyes

   - The pride of life.

4. Read Romans 12:2. Would you describe this season in your Christian walk as more conforming or transforming? Explain your answer.

5. Provide an example of a lie the world promotes that some in the church have adopted as a belief.

Day 3: Entangled

Daily Devotion

In Brazil there grows a common plant which forest-dwellers call the matador or "murderer." Its slender stem creeps along the ground, but no sooner does it meet a vigorous tree, than it sends out an entangling tentacle, which cleaves and climbs up the tree, at intervals sending out arm-like tendrils that further entangle the tree. As the "murderer" ascends, these ligatures grow larger and their clasp becomes tighter. Up and up the rogue vine climbs until the last loftiest spire is gained and fettered. Then, as if in triumph, the parasite shoots a huge, flowery head above the strangled summit, and there from the dead tree's crown, scatters its seed to begin its entangling work again. In a similar way everyday affairs can subtly entangle soldiers of Christ, in effect neutralizing their effectiveness in the ongoing spiritual war with the world, the flesh and the devil. John Piper says when a Christian soldier's "evenings and days off (begin to be) filled up with harmless, enjoyable diversions… the whole feel changes. The radical urgency fades. The wartime mentality shifts to a peacetime mentality. The lifestyle starts to get cushy. The all-consuming singleness of vision evaporates." Spurgeon adds that "Many of God's children are in this condition -- entangled, surrounded, captive, held fast!"[x]

Digging Deeper

1. Read and write out 2 Timothy 2:4.

2. Paul points out that soldiers don't concern themselves with non-military matters: they have a job to do. Nor do they worry about issues unrelated to their specific mission. In other words, a Roman soldier would not be distracted by "civilian" concerns: entertainment, politics, or weather, for example. Instead, his focus was entirely on fulfilling the orders of his commander. In this word picture, Christ is the one who has enlisted Timothy. His goal was not the trivial issues of life, but the mission for which God had called him.[xi]

   What are some of the "affairs of this life" that have you distracted and preoccupied?

3. How can the pleasures of this world work to "lull" the Christian to sleep?

4. What are some ways we can keep a healthy balance in enjoying some of the pleasures of this world, without becoming attached to them? Use Scripture to support your answer.

5. Are there any "murderous vines" in your life that need to be removed?

Day 4: Socially Acceptable Sin

Daily Devotion

The Christians to whom Peter wrote, faced the same temptations believers encounter today. Roman culture celebrated carnality and flaunted their sexual immorality. Sin was acceptable and its presence surrounded these believers no matter where they turned. It was necessary to continually resist the temptation to participate, and strive to live holy lives.

Digging Deeper

1. Paul writes in Galatians 5:19-21 (NLT):

   When you follow the desires of your sinful nature, the results are very clear: sexual immorality, impurity, lustful pleasures, idolatry, sorcery, hostility, quarreling, jealousy, outbursts of anger, selfish ambition, dissension, division, envy, drunkenness, wild parties, and other sins like these. Let me tell you again, as I have before, that anyone living that sort of life will not inherit the Kingdom of God.

   Which of these sins listed above are widely accepted in today's culture?

2. What did Jesus teach in the Parable of the Rich Fool in Luke 12:13-21?

3. What are some ways the culture entices us to participate in the sin of covetousness and greed?

4. As certain sins become more widely accepted in the culture, why do they become more dangerous for the believer?

5. Read 1 Thessalonians 4:3-8. Using these verses, how would you explain to a new believer that sexual purity is imperative for pleasing God?

Day 5: Living Unsettled

1. Which of the four days this week challenged you the most?

2. Write a paragraph summarizing what you have learned about the unsettled life.

3. What key verse will you seek to memorize and hide in your heart?

4. Moving forward, how will you apply what you have learned?

5. Take some time to consider your answers and compose a prayer that reflects what God's Word has spoken to you.

Week 6
A Lifestyle to Maintain
1 Peter 2:12

Lord, may our words and deeds be true,
As people of the light,
And help us as we follow You
To always do what's right.

Sper

Week 6: A Lifestyle to Maintain

Having your conduct honorable among the Gentiles, that when they speak against you as evildoers, they may, by your good works which they observe, glorify God —2 Peter 2:12

Study Focus

What does your lifestyle say to the world around you? What is the overall flavor of your life? Peter is challenging us to *honorable* conduct. The word *honorable* is rich in context in the Greek. In its simplest definition, the word *kalos* means "beautiful". It carries with its meaning the idea of an attractively good life that inspires other to embrace what is lovely.

In other words, our lives should be attractive to the unbelieving people in our spheres of influence who observe our everyday lives. The word "observe" used in this verse speaks to a long-term observation. Even if unbelievers reject Christ or the Bible, they should note something different and good about us that can't be denied.

You may be unaware, but unbelievers are watching your life.

- They see how you react to things at work.

- They observe how you talk about others.

- They watch how you deal with problems.

- They note how you treat your family.

Peter recognizes in the harsh environment that surrounds the believer, good works will not immediately convert the lost. In fact, just the opposite may happen. People may become convicted by our lives, jealous, and may even mock or slander us, or tempt us to ruin our witness. When evildoers speak against us, our responsibility is merely to maintain our witness and to live for the glory of God. Although believers are to lead honorable lives, we are not called to compromise, or do whatever it takes to appease the world, in order to not be criticized.

This week will not be easy. The obedience Peter is asking for cannot be met in the energy of our own strength. It cannot be achieved by trying hard. At the time of Peter's writing, Christians were being martyred for their faith—they would walk to their deaths demonstrating a deep faith in God with love and forgiveness for those who would take their physical lives. They knew what was at stake, and clearly understood their mission had been accomplished. This world was not their home.

In order to live this life, we have to draw upon our great love for God, our deep belief in His Word, and complete dependence upon His Holy Spirit. We must be bold and courageous and remember our mission. We must forsake the convenience of our lives, and remember the One who sacrificed His.

Day 1: Adorning the Gospel

Daily Devotion

Believers are called to live the beautiful life. In doing so they are to adorn the truth of the gospel.

"To adorn it is to honor it, and make it honorable before all. It implies that we commend it by being ourselves an illustration of its meaning, and by evincing to all its spirit and efficacy. We are to prove the excellence of the doctrine by showing, in our own case, what it can do in the hands of the Holy Spirit to reform the world. The doctrine is good or otherwise, according to its practical results. If it accomplishes what it aims to, it is beyond expression valuable and glorious. That it can and does, is just the thing which God leaves for His people to prove by their lives. Hence, they must live so as to hold forth the excellence, beauty and power, of the gospel."[xii]

Digging Deeper

1. The word "adorn" comes from the Greek word *kosmeo* which primarily means to "arrange or to put in order." Imagine the amount of time you spend to arrange the perfect outfit for a wedding or important occasion. In the same way, you are to adorn yourself with godliness: *ordering and arranging your life to properly display what it is that you believe.*

   According to Colossians 3:12-14 what are some things we can "put on" to adorn the doctrine of God?

2. List the characteristics of the Titus 2 woman in Titus 2:3-5. When women are growing in the Word of God, and yielding to the Holy Spirit, they are able to walk in obedience to these verses. In doing so, they bring fame to God in the process. According to Titus 2:5, what happens when a woman fails to live this way?

3. What does it mean to blaspheme the Word of God by the way we live?

4. What does 1 Peter 3:3-4 teach concerning women and the adornment of the doctrine of God? Why are these qualities attractive to the unbelieving world?

5. Read Ephesians 5:1-2. We are to be the fragrance of Christ. What does that practically look like as we seek to adorn the gospel?

Day 2: Where the Rubber Meets the Road

Daily Devotion

The phrase *"where the rubber meets the road"* is used to describe the point at which a theory or idea is put to a practical test. Perhaps some of the most difficult commands for the Christian are found in Romans chapter 12. It has been appropriately nicknamed the chapter where the rubber meets the road for the believer in Christ. These commands are not suggestions, they are not nice ideas or possible theories. Believers are expected to live out these truths in practice.

Digging Deeper

1. In Romans 12:1, we learn that as a result of the mercy shown us by God, we are called in verses 3-21 to model love in our relationships. What did Jesus teach concerning love in Luke 6:32-36?

2. When in the past or currently has Jesus asked you to love a person who is not easy to love?

3. Read Romans 12:9-21. What do you learn about living the "beautiful life" from these verses?

4. Paul describes love in action. Which of these commands do you find the most difficult? Explain why.

- Blessing those who persecute you

- Living at peace with everyone

- Not taking revenge

- Associating with people of low status

5. Christians were being fiercely persecuted and murdered for their faith at the time of Peter's writing. Peter is pleading with them to maintain their witness. Is it ever right to respond with evil for evil? Why or why not?

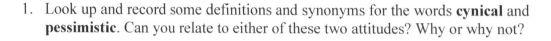

Day 3: Evil Doers

Daily Devotion

Why do the wicked prosper? It is a question that if not addressed, can cause us to become disappointed with God. We have a hard time believing that God is a God of justice, when day after day we see nothing but injustices all around us. When evil appears to be winning, the Christian must avoid growing cynical and pessimistic. A defeatist attitude can easily set in: "If we can't beat them, we'll join them."

Digging Deeper

1. Look up and record some definitions and synonyms for the words **cynical** and **pessimistic**. Can you relate to either of these two attitudes? Why or why not?

2. Read Psalm 37. How do evil doers cause us to fret?

3. What are we to do instead of fretting?

   - Psalm 37:3

   - Psalm 37:4

   - Psalm 37:5

   - Psalm 37:7

   - Psalm 37:8

4. We must cling tightly to the promises of God. Study Psalm 37 and journal the promises God has given regarding the wicked.

5. Prayer is powerful. We can stand courageously for the Word of God and pray for His favor and protection. We can pray for him to thwart the plans of evil doers. Pray Psalm 21 and rejoice in the strength of God!

Day 4: Not Without Hope

Daily Devotion

Paul wrote to the Thessalonian believers: "But I do not want you to be ignorant, brethren, concerning those who have fallen asleep, lest you sorrow as others who have no hope (1 Thessalonians 4:13)." While the context of this verse relates to physical death, it also applies to the sorrow we experience as we grieve the loss of our nation's love for God, and respect for His values:

- The loss of marriage between a man and a woman
- The loss of the unborn baby in the womb
- The loss of prayer in schools
- The loss of civility in relationships
- The loss of justice in our court systems
- The loss of morality in America

But we are not to sorrow as those who have no hope. Hope must remain alive and well in our hearts because our hope is not in this world, it is in God.

Digging Deeper

1. According to Romans 15:4, what are some of the reasons the Scriptures were written? Are you finding comfort and hope in the Word of God? Why or why not?

2. What does Romans 15:13 teach us about hope?

3. If hope abounds in faith by the power of the Holy Spirit, why do Christians become hopeless?

4. In Psalm 71, the writer chooses joy. Write out and memorize Psalm 71. Declare it every morning and choose joy!

5. Read 1 Peter 1:3-8. Why should the believer's hope always be alive?

Day 5: Living Unsettled

1. Which of the four days this week challenged you the most?

2. Write a paragraph summarizing what you have learned about the unsettled life.

3. What key verse will you seek to memorize and hide in your heart?

4. Moving forward, how will you apply what you have learned?

5. Take some time to consider your answers and compose a prayer that reflects what God's Word has spoken to you.

Week 7
The Day of Visitation
1 Peter 2:12

To such a salvation our heed we must give,
Lest drifting away or neglecting we live.
Christ now as our life, future ruling with Him,
We'll miss if we miss this salvation within.

So great a salvation, Ye Saints of the Lord
https://www.hymnal.net/en/hymn/h/1129

Week 7: The Day of Visitation

...Glorify God in the day of visitation—1 Peter 2:12

Study Focus

An examination of the Greek word translated "visitation" reveals that its use here may have two meanings – one temporal (earthly visitation) and the other eschatological (final visitation or Judgment Day). Each of these meanings can have two purposes – visitation for blessing or for punishment.

What did Peter mean when he said that those who observe our good deeds will glorify God in the day of visitation? What is the day of visitation? Scholars believe it can refer to one of two possibilities. It may refer to God's visitation in saving these pagans, implying that unbelievers who slander Christians may come to salvation as a result of observing the Christian's good works, or it may refer to the account they will have to give to Him who is ready to judge the living and the dead. This may be what Peter is talking about concerning the Day of Judgment in chapter 4:

They will give an account to Him who is ready to judge the living and the dead. For the time has come for judgment to begin at the house of God; and if it begins with us first, what will be the end of those who do not obey the gospel of God? Now "If the righteous one is scarcely saved, where will the ungodly and the sinner appear?" Therefore let those who suffer according to the will of God commit their souls to Him in doing good, as to a faithful Creator—1 Peter 4:5, 17-19

It is possible to take both references into account. God will vindicate the Christian's righteous behavior, apart from what happens to those who persecute them. Some unbelievers will get saved before that day because they observed the good deeds of Christians whom they persecuted. In doing so, they will glorify God for His saving grace and for the faithfulness of His people. Others will stand before God with every excuse for their unbelief.

As pilgrims we keep both proposed days of visitation in view: the salvation of the believer *now*, and judgment in the *future*. No matter which scenario plays out, our responsibility remains the same: to continue to witness and bring glory to God with our lives. We should seek to persuade those who are on the road to condemnation, to receive God's mercy before it is too late.

Day 1: Today is the Day

Daily Devotion

Every person will spend eternity in one of two places, heaven or hell. Many who have heard the good news of Jesus Christ reject His offer of forgiveness in order to live unrighteously. The Book of Romans is clear to teach that men suppress the truth of God in order to live unrighteously. When God calls us to share the gospel, we want to respond in prompt obedience, well aware that today may be the day of salvation for the unbeliever He has asked us to witness to.

Digging Deeper

1. Read 2 Corinthians 6:1-2. Why is "today" the day of salvation?

2. Read Luke 19:41-44. What did Jesus mean when He said that Jerusalem "did not know the time of their visitation?"

3. Share the day of your visitation. What caused you to believe and trust in Jesus Christ as your Lord and Savior?

4. Why are Christians sometimes the reason that unbelievers are stumbled and miss Jesus?

5. How can the knowledge that the goodness of God leads to repentance (Romans 2:4) help us in our evangelistic efforts?

Day 2: The Judgment Seat of Christ

Daily Devotion

While believers are not judged according to their sin, there are rewards given for faithfulness in the Christian life and loss of rewards for unfaithfulness. We are not merely in this race to run, but to win! "The Lord is absolutely worthy of our obedience and service, whether we ever personally profit from it or not. Nevertheless, the Lord is a rewarder of those who seek Him and He commands us to seek His rewards as well! And when we really think about it, "Hearing our Master say, 'Well done' will not simply be for our pleasure but for His!"[xiii]

Digging Deeper

1. Read 2 Corinthians 5:9-11. What is the aim God calls believers to in 2 Corinthians 5:9?

2. Kay Smith, in her book, *Pleasing God* provides us with further insight.

   To please someone means to delight, to satisfy, or to gratify. When our aim is to please God, then we begin to weigh all our actions in the light of whether or not those actions are pleasing to Him. And this is not something we do just out of obedience. We do these things out of an attitude of love. There is a big difference between the two. If you have children, you know that they can obey you by taking out the trash, while griping all the way. But if one morning the trash has been emptied just to please you, you know the difference – and God does too.

   Are your works for Christ motivated by love or performance? Explain your answer.

3. Read 1 Corinthians 3:9-15. How will the believer's works be evaluated for reward?

4. 1 Corinthians 3:9-15 reveal a sober reality: Some Christians will be resurrected with but with little to show for the time they spent on earth—they "will be saved, but only as one escaping through the flames." Give some examples of the works of a believer that will burn and suffer loss.

5. The New Testament describes as many as five different crowns which will be given to believers for various works of faithfulness, obedience, discipline, and love. They help us to gain a good understanding of what sojourns and pilgrims are to be doing in their time on earth. Look up each Scripture and draw a line connecting the appropriate crown with its rewarded behavior.

CROWN

The Imperishable Crown
(1 Corinthians 9:25)

The Crown of Rejoicing
(Philippians 4:1, 1 Thessalonians 2:19)

The Crown of Righteousness
(2 Timothy 4:8)

The Crown of Glory
(1 Peter 5:4)

The Crown of Life
(Revelation 2:10, James 1:12)

WORKS

Faithfulness to Christ in persecution or martyrdom

Determination, discipline and victory in the Christian life

Faithfully representing Christ in a position of leadership

Pouring oneself into others in evangelism and discipleship

To all who long for His appearing

Day 3: The Great White Throne Judgment

Daily Devotion

Nothing is as sobering as the truth of the Great White Throne Judgment. If we decide to settle in this life, we will forget the terrifying eternity that awaits those who reject Christ's forgiveness, choosing eternal damnation. This reality should cause us to better understand why we are here, and to have compassion and love for the lost.

Digging Deeper

1. Read Revelation 20:11-15, describe what will take place at the Great White Throne Judgment.

2. What do we learn about Paul's heart for the Jews in Romans 9:1-5?

3. How can believers grow callous and numb regarding the plight of unbelievers?

4. How should the reality of hell impact our journey here on earth?

5. What are some practical ways we can nurture a passion for the lost?

Day 4: Homesick for Heaven

Daily Devotion

Hopefully, by this time in the study, you have recognized that much of your "unsettledness" is a result of being homesick. As a faithful believer in Christ, you will never "fit in" and for the time being you are homeless. You will always feel out of place because you are a stranger and an alien. Disappointment and discouragement will be a continuing experience— if you fail to identify it for what it truly is – homesickness.

"As a Christian, your sense of homelessness and homesickness is normal. If you've been fighting it, stop! Embracing your homelessness as a disciple is to embrace freedom. If you don't burden your worldly experiences with the expectations of making them your home, their disappointments won't be so heavy, and you'll be able to lay aside the weight of cynicism."[xiv]

Digging Deeper

1. What have you learned about yourself and your temporary journey here on earth? Are you ready to embrace the "unsettled" life? Why or why not?

2. In what ways, can the truths of Colossians 3:1 and 2 Corinthians 4:16-18, keep us from being homesick?

3. Our failing, physical bodies tell us that we are not home. The fallen world subjects our bodies to disease, disability, aging, and death. But one day we will be at home in our resurrected bodies. What does Paul teach us about our new bodies in 1 Corinthians 15:42-44 and in 2 Corinthians 5:1-8?

4. What encouragement do you receive from Revelation 21:1-4?

5. While we lose those we love in this physical life, we have the hope of reunion in heaven. Our hearts ache to be with those we love. Yet, while we are here we do not want to waste our time and energy on the things of this world. Our goal is to take as many people as we can to heaven with us. As a result of this study, what will you do to take more people to heaven with you?

Homesick for Heaven

Saying goodbye to those that we love,
Is the hardest thing to do.
But I've set my mind on things above
And I know when this life is through
I'll move to a city where no one will cry,
No disappointments, no sad good-byes,
No more dying, I'm Packed and ready to move.

Refrain.
Homesick for heaven, my heart is longing to go.
Homesick for heaven, loved ones awaiting I know
I've missed them so....
I'm homesick for heaven
And I can't just wait to go home.

I closed my eyes and I see a place,
Far beyond my wildest dreams.
Where heartaches aren't welcome and tears cannot stay
And pain will give way to peace.
Where life is forever and good things won't end,
Death will conquer never again,
I'm more than ready to hear heaven's choir start to sing.

Refrain...
I want to go home
I can't wait to go home
Refrain...
Homesick for heaven.

Jim Brady Trio

https://www.youtube.com/watch?v=brJyeTokn7E&list=RDbrJyeTokn7E

Day 5: Living Unsettled

1. Which of the four days this week challenged you the most?

2. Write a paragraph summarizing what you have learned about the unsettled life.

3. What key verse will you seek to memorize and hide in your heart?

4. Moving forward, how will you apply what you have learned?

5. Take some time to consider your answers and compose a prayer that reflects what God's Word has spoken to you.

About the Author

Margy Hill's passion and calling for women's ministry led her to start the Women's Ministry Connection, where she encourages and exhorts women leaders in ministry. God has given her the opportunity to speak into the lives of women of all ages and church backgrounds. She loves to teach and share her passion for the Word of God, stirring women to a deeper and more abundant relationship with Jesus, encouraging and equipping them to walk in the fullness of their callings.

Her gift for writing has led her to publish several Bible studies to help women develop a desire to dig deeper into the Word of God. With challenging questions and everyday application, her studies have been widely used throughout churches in the United States.

Margy speaks and teaches for women's conferences, retreats and seminars, and is also known for her "Hope for the Hurting Heart" training workshops designed to equip women to counsel confidently from the Word of God. She recently graduated with her Bachelor's in Biblical Studies and is pursuing her Masters in Christian Counseling. Margy resides in Oceanside, California and is blessed to be able to serve with her husband who is a teaching pastor, gifted in apologetics. He is also a contributing writer, often adding excellent commentary to Margy's studies.

For more information on Margy's ministry, visit her website at www.wmconnection.org. All of Margy's studies are featured on Amazon. Group discounts are available by contacting Margy at mhill@wmconnection.org.

END NOTES

[i] John Piper, *The Roots of Endurance, Invincible Perseverance in the Lives of John Newton,* Charles Simeon, and William Wilberforce, (Wheaton, IL: Crossway Publishers, 2002), 18.

[ii] Waldie, Dr. D. Lance, *Perfect Love Casts Out Fear,* http://www.harvestbiblechurch.net/blog/perfect-love-casts-out-fear

[iii] Jerry Bridges, *Trusting God: Even When Life Hurts,* (Colorado Springs, CO: Nav Press, 1989).

[iv] Jason Helopoulos, "Do You Feel Tension in the Christian Life"? https://www.thegospelcoalition.org/blogs/kevin-deyoung/do-you-feel-tension-in-the-christian-life/

[v] Johannes P. Louw and Eugene Albert Nida, *Greek-English Lexicon of the New Testament: Based on Semantic Domains* (New York: United Bible Societies, 1996), 132.

[vi] Anna Bachinsky, "God Doesn't Want You to be Comfortable", https://daughterbydesign.wordpress.com/2013/04/24/god-doesnt-want-you-to-be-comfortable/

[vii] Ellery Sadler, "The Art of Holding Loosely, May 11, 2015, https://relevantmagazine.com/life/art-holding-loosely

[viii] https://www.christianitytoday.com/pastors/2011/summer/bubblewrapped.html

[ix] Rick Renner, "Abstain From Fleshly Lusts," https://renner.org/abstain-from-fleshly-lusts/

[x] Precept Austin, http://www.preceptaustin.org/are_you_entangled

[xi] Bible Reference, https://www.bibleref.com/2-Timothy/2/2-Timothy-2-4.html

[xii] Charles Finney, "Adorning the Gospel," December 5, 1855, https://www.gospeltruth.net/1855OE/551205_adorning_doctrine.htm

[xiii] Randy Alcorn, *Heaven,* (Carol Stream, IL: Tyndale House Publishers, 2004)

[xiv] John Piper, "Live Homeless, Homesick, and Free, (March 2015) https://www.desiringgod.org/articles/live-homeless-homesick-and-free

Made in the USA
Columbia, SC
07 June 2018